SORRY, WE DON'T USE CONSULTANTS

HOW TO KEEP GETTING PAID BY HAPPY CLIENTS

BY GEOFF GARDEN

DEDICATION

This book is dedicated to two very special people:

Judy – my amazing wife who has been
my inspiration for 40 years

Bruce Thorne – who rescued me from Corporate life
and freed my *"inner"* entrepreneur

ABOUT GEOFF

With over thirty years of business experience in North America, Europe and Asia, Geoff has developed a wide general perspective and a particular expertise in helping clients find and take advantage of new opportunity. He has a deep understanding of global business practices, coupled with the ability to help clients move the vision they have for the future into a revenue generating reality. Also, during his corporate career, Geoff hired and worked with hundreds of consultants and is therefore uniquely positioned to offer them counsel with a view from both *"sides of the table".*

PREFACE

There are a lot of very bad people in the world who call themselves consultants. This is both a good and bad thing for you. It's good because the competitive bar is very low. It's bad because, as a result of the damage these people have caused, clients hate consultants almost as much as lawyers and life insurance salesmen. This is true, and yet, good lawyers and life insurance salesmen make a ton of money and people need them even if they don't want them. The same is true for good consultants.

I do not presume to have all the answers. This book has been written to be a thought provoking exercise for great business advisors. Getting paid, on a long term basis, by a happy client, is the ultimate A+ report card for any consultant.

It means that:

- The client believes they continue to get real value.
- If you are prepared to stick around it probably also means that you are getting more out of it than just the money.

"Loyal, interesting, successful clients who are happy to keep paying me" sounds like a good deal all around.

CONTENTS

Introduction – "It's not rocket science" —————————— 11

CHAPTERS

1. Setting the Stage: The Client's View ———————— 13
2. "What do you want to do?" ——————————————— 19
3. "What do you do?" ——————————————————————— 29
4. "How do you do that?" ———————————————————— 41
5. "How does it work?" ————————————————————— 47
6. Continuing to get paid ——————————————————— 69
7. Notes ————————————————————————————————— 85

INTRODUCTION

"It's not rocket science"

I believe that success as a business advisor comes as a result of being able to do three things very well:

1. Clearly and simply explaining the value that you deliver

2. Creating a process that ensures you deliver that value every time

3. Developing enough trust and credibility with clients that they want to keep you around to help them as they grow

This is because, in my experience, clients want to know three things:

1. What do you do and why should I care?
2. How do you do that?
3. How do I know you will actually deliver?

Six years ago I created the Dreamland Program™ specifically to help myself and my colleagues answer these three client questions as we worked to build our business advisory firm The Pace Network (www.thepacenetwork.com). Since then Dreamland™, coupled with a great stewardship process, has been a key driver of our ability to get and retain great clients. This book will take you through the Dreamland™ approach and help you to:

1. Identify and articulate the value you deliver to clients

2. Understand the importance of having a defined process behind what you do as it relates to convincing clients that you will really deliver that value

3. Create your own value proposition and the underlying process

Along the way, we will also discuss how to create an approach that ensures you will continue to be paid by happy clients!

Nothing we are going to talk about is rocket science. The key to being a successful business advisor simply lies in understanding what "Value" is from your client's perspective and then delivering that on an ongoing basis. The problem arises when we take the time to create what we think is a great solution and then go and try to sell that to people – without taking the time to see things from their perspective first. What we will be going through will help you to avoid that mistake.

It turns out that the used car salesman we all laugh at got it exactly right with the famous question:

"What do I have to do to get you in this car today?"

Which can simply be translated as:

"Just tell me what it is that you need and I will try to match it up with what I can deliver. If I can do that – and explain to you clearly how that will work – then why wouldn't you buy it from me?"

I believe that a the ability to get and retain loyal clients comes from the **"The successful communication of real value to the prospect."**

The objective of this book is to help you get that done and continue to "get paid by happy clients"

CHAPTER ONE

SETTING THE STAGE – THE CLIENT'S VIEW

What Does the Client Think?

So let's look at some quotes that give us a bit of insight around what a lot of clients think consultants do:

"How many consultants does it take to change a light bulb? We don't know. They never get past the feasibility study".

Unknown Author

"A consultant is someone who saves his client almost enough to pay his fee".

Arnold H. Glasgow

"Some consultants are like the bottom half of a double boiler: They get all heated up but don't know what's cooking.

Unknown Author

"Hiring consultants to conduct studies can be an excellent means of turning problems into gold - your problems, their gold".

Unknown Author

You can see these as sadly amusing or cynical, but all the best comedy is funny because it has a grain of truth in it. Just listen to George Carlin talk about our "Stuff" and Jerry Seinfeld built his career on making observations about life. We thought it was funny because we recognized ourselves in it and it rang true.

But, in the final analysis, it doesn't matter what we think – what the client thinks is the important thing. So if you assume that all clients think this way about consultants then you can't really go wrong. If they do, then you will be addressing the issue and if they don't then you will just look even better – no downside.

What these consultant stories are really talking about is the perception of the lack of value being delivered: Consultants:

- "Show up, ask me to tell them my problems, write me a report that recaps the conversation, give me a bill and leave".

- "Show up with preconceived notions about my business with a canned process for how they are going to help me get it right".

- "Think they are knights in shining armor, showing up to save the day".

- "Can't demonstrate any tangible value they have to deliver to me".

- "Don't have any business experience but want to tell me how to run mine".

- "Of the last two I dealt with, one was actually a crook and the other was simply useless."

The sad thing is that all of the above are comments I have heard directly from business owners and that's why I never refer to myself as a consultant –

Quick Tip: refer to yourself as a Business Advisor not a Consultant. If the client denigrates Consultants you can say "Thank god I'm not one of those – I'm a Business Advisor". This may sound goofy but it's actually supposed to, because the point is to get them to ask you what the heck the difference is… we will cover the answer to that later. If they don't bring it up then you make sure you get the question by finding an excuse to tell them you are an Advisor not a Consultant.

But what's really behind these comments is the sad fact that consultants can't clearly explain – in a way that resonates with the client - what they do, how they do it and how it works. In other words, from client's perspective:

"What do you do? How do you do that? Why should I care? How does it work?"

Or even more directly –

- **"What value are you going to bring to me?"**
- **"Why should I believe you will actually deliver it?"**
- **"What proof do you have that you can do this?"**
- **"Is there more behind this than just another empty promise?"**

So now we have set the table, let's move onto what we can do to fix this and secure the future.

CHAPTER TWO
"WHAT DO YOU WANT TO DO?"

What do you want to do?

It would be a sad thing to be very successful getting and keeping clients you didn't like working with, and doing things for them that you don't want to do. So the first step in answering the question **"What do you do?"** is to figure out **what it is you actually want to do** – for the rest of your life.

Answering this question is a really important element in getting and keeping happy clients. That's because:

- If you are doing what you love to do then you will continue to focus on it, have high energy around it and clients will love you for it

- It turns out that we are usually really great at doing the things that we love to do. So if we can figure out what those things are, and focus on them with clients, then everyone wins

(One potential problem we need to avoid, however, is that because it does come easily to us we tend to discount how valuable it is for the rest of the world – our clients. We will deal with this issue later in the book.)

My view has always been that there are only three elements that matter in answering this question, and they are **Fun, Fulfillment and Personal Wealth.**

FUN:

The Oxford English dictionary defines fun as "A behavior or activity that is intended purely for amusement or entertainment".

As we grew up we were told we had to eat our vegetables before we could get any ice cream. Then, as we started careers, we were told that everyone has stuff in their jobs that they don't like to do but – "that's life". As entrepreneurs, we can figure out what we love to do, what is "fun" for us to do – and just do that. Calories notwithstanding, we get to eat ice cream all the time – without having to put up with any Brussel Sprouts - and work on things that "are intended purely for our amusement or entertainment". As noted above, the really good news is that the stuff that is fun for us to do is always the stuff that we turn out to be best at doing, and adds the most value for our clients. How do you figure out what is fun for you? The answer will be unique for each of us and I suggest you start out by answering the following questions for yourself:

- **What gives me energy?** There are days when we are busy all day and yet we have more energy at the end of the day than when we started. These are the days that produced Fun and Fulfillment. This is where we want to spend our lives. Think about some of those days and what you were doing. For example:

    - The type of work you were doing
    - The type of people you were with
    - The issues you conquered
    - The results you achieved

- **What robs me of energy?** Sometimes it's easier to figure out what "it isn't" rather than "what it is" so in contrast to the first question, what are the things you dread having to do? Clues would be that you procrastinate when you have to do them and you feel like a kid when you finish them: "Hey! I just finished my homework and now I get to go outside and play".

- **If the money didn't matter, what would I do to help business people "for free"?** For me, the answer to this is "Show up, sing and leave." Which means getting connected with someone on a problem or opportunity and helping them to find a creative way to deal with it. I just want to facilitate, participate and leave. I don't want to write the report or run the resulting project. Doing this type of work, and helping people create something new or solve a problem, produces a huge amount of fun and fulfillment for me. If creating the personal wealth didn't matter it's what I would do all day long for free. The answer for each of us will be different and the nature of the activity could be:

    - Analysis
    - Project work
    - Creative work
    - Coaching
    - Fixing or creating systems and processes
    - Technical writing
    - Marketing work

Who is/was my best client and why?

- Type of person
- Type of company
- Type of work

What was my best deal or project and why?

- Nature of the work
- The role I played
- The help I gave

What gives me confidence?

- Typically things that come naturally and need very little preparation by me and may keep me awake at night as I go through them – because of excitement and anticipation

What steals my confidence?

- Typically things that require me to prepare and research and may keep me awake at night as I go through them – because of fear of failure

These questions are by no means comprehensive but are designed to make you think about the answer and debate it with yourself or other people who know you well.

Figuring out what's fun for you is the single most critical element. When you get that part right, Fulfillment and Personal Wealth will follow.

Life is relatively short so why spend it doing something painful? Remember, to quote Carly Simon "These are the good old days" – shame on us if we don't make the most of them.

FULFILLMENT:

The Oxford English dictionary defines fulfillment as "The happiness achieved as a result of fully developing one's full potential or the satisfaction of performing your duty as promised".

So my definition would be that, while fun is getting to eat ice cream and not cabbage, fulfillment is the **"Selfish satisfaction we get from helping other people and doing something worthwhile".**

Fulfillment comes from the value we deliver in whatever it is we do. Ask yourself the following questions in order to think through where fulfillment comes from for you:

- **What are the three client/work related things that you have accomplished that delivered the highest level of personal satisfaction and pride such as:**
    - Impact on people
    - Impact on outcome
    - Creation of something new, *i.e. it didn't exist in the world before*

- **Why was each one personally fulfilling for you?**
    - Appreciation from the client
    - Personal growth for you

- **What skills, talent and ability did you use in getting each one done?**

    - Technical skill
    - General Management skill
    - Application of general life experience

PERSONAL WEALTH:

This is defined by me as the amount of money you need to have in order to make the Fun and Fulfillment go around today and secure your financial future for tomorrow.

This is not a book about financial planning or budgeting – so you will not be getting any advice from me in that direction. Thinking about the amount of wealth you need is important in our context, for one reason: **Work/Life balance.**

Once we have gone through the process of figuring out the type of work we will be doing (and how we will get clients to keep paying us to do it) the next thing is to figure out how much of it we want to do. Whether you are on your own, have partners or employees, you get to choose how much work, and of what type, you will do.

When figuring out the work life balance, I suggest people take the following simple approach:

Ask yourself this question:

"How much money do I HAVE to make in order to cover my personal "burn rate" and have any kind of basic lifestyle – no Lamborghini in the driveway but we can go out to dinner and a movie when we want to"?

We are asking this question in order to determine the "floor" amount of revenue you need. The answer is usually a pleasant surprise for most people because it is generally much lower than they thought it would be and provides some peace of mind. It also sets you up for the next question which is:

"How much money would I like to make in order to do what I want to do today (including the Lamborghini if that's on the list) and establish financial independence and security for the future?"

Going through this exercise "brackets" the financial situation and also makes you think about what your bucket list goals for life are, along with the longer term security requirement.

To help you figure out what you need the money for, you can complete the following three lists:

My Life:

1. **The Things I Love to Do**
2. **The Things I Hate to Do**
3. **The Things I Still Want From Life**

Doing this will give you an idea of what you will need money for (love to do) – so that you can do it, such as travel etc. It will also give you an idea of what you will need money for (hate to do), so you can pay someone else to do it for you, such as painting the house, cutting the grass and cleaning the gutters. *(Those are from my list!)*

Now we have given some thought to:

- What we want to do and why
- How much money we need and why

Let's move on to how we are going to get the work we want and get happy clients to pay us forever.

CHAPTER THREE

"WHAT DO YOU DO?"

Dreamland™: Vision to Reality

I promised that this would not be rocket science and it really isn't. Let's recap what we have done so far vs. the goal:

Goal:

Continuing to get paid by happy clients

Step 1:

- Realizing that it is pointless to get hired to do something you don't like doing

Step 2:

- How to figure out what you actually want to get hired to do

Now we move onto making it happen:

THE DREAMLAND™ PROGRAM.

I created Dreamland™ about six years ago when I got a phone call one evening from a former colleague who was working for a bank in New York. After catching up for a few minutes, she said "Geoff, I'm sick of working in Banking and I have decided to get out and become a Life Coach". "Great," I said, "Let's assume I am your first prospect. Tell me what you are going to do for me." Nancy started talking. Five minutes later, I interrupted her and said "Hey Nancy, you have been talking for five minutes and I still don't know what you do and what's in it for me."

I had a white board behind me so I put her on speaker, got up and wrote the following on the board:

1. Idea
2. Tools
3. Process
4. Content
5. Pricing
6. Packaging

I explained to Nancy what I had written on the board and what I meant by each of them:

Idea:

- What is the basic concept of your program? What is the essence of the value I will get from it?

Tools:

- What are the tools you will use to guide me through your program? (Do you use exercises, plans, coaching tools etc.?)

Process:

- What is the process used behind each tool and how does it work?

Content:

- Is there any content that accompanies your program such as a book, CD, video?

Pricing:

- What is your business model? How much will you charge me and how will it work? One-time fee, ongoing retainer, hourly?

Packaging:

- I told Nancy that, once we had the answers to the previous points, the packaging would follow.

After we had chatted about each one I said "Ok, start thinking about it and call me back when you have the answers." About two weeks later, Nancy called me back and walked me through what she had come up with. It wasn't perfect but I wound up with a much clearer picture of what she would be doing for me as a client and the value I would receive from her. An additional benefit was that, as she had been considering the answers to the questions, she had clarified the program for herself and refined a number of her business plan elements. Nancy never actually became a life coach, but the difference in the "pitch" I received from her before and after what we had gone through, made me think that perhaps we had discovered something. I started to work on the process and refined it into the Dreamland Program™.

Dreamland™ is the foundation for how you will get hired and continue to get paid by happy clients.

The program will help you to define the value you bring to your clients and create the program for delivering it. Here is how it works:

What do you do? – The Value Question

Modern business has done itself a major disservice by creating way too much business-speak. As noted earlier, "Value Added" is a prime example. While that is true, it is also true that it is the ability to communicate true value and deliver it on a consistent basis that gets and keeps you hired. So the first step in Dreamland™ is designed to help you cut through the business-speak fog and get right to the heart of what is important to your target client, identifying the absolute pure essence of the value that you deliver. How do we get that done? Well, part of a non-rocket science approach involves not reinventing any wheels so Dreamland™ doesn't do that. We use our own version of the fabled Elevator Speech, as follows:

The Elevator:

Imagine you are in one of the two fabulous suites on the top floor of Caesars Palace in Las Vegas. You are getting into the elevator to go out to dinner and a show (not gambling of course…). Just as the door is closing a guy sticks his arm in, opens it and gets in.

He has bourbon on the rocks in his hand, is rumpled, bent, folded, spindled and mutilated, jaded, bored and cynical. He has heard everything, seen everything, doesn't think he will ever learn anything new and doesn't believe anything he is told. The best salespeople in the world are constantly calling on him and he has seen every pitch in the book. Oh, and by the way, he just happens to be your perfect prospect.

He doesn't care about you or what you do but his choices are to talk to you or just watch the floor numbers count down from 75 to L – talking to you wins by a thin margin… So he looks at you and says **"What do you do?"** Of course he doesn't really care what you do and doesn't expect to hear anything new or interesting – it's just that you are marginally more compelling than the elevator numbers. So, your challenge is to hit him with an incredibly powerful, outrageous and only just barely true statement of what you do and the value it delivers. And you have to deliver it in 5 seconds or less.

The point of this first exercise in the Dreamland™ process is to force you to identify the pure essence of the value you deliver to your target client. In order to do that you have to think carefully about those people, what would be valuable to them and why, the equivalent of the car salesman question "what do I have to do to get you in this car today?" This is a useful exercise in itself since it makes you consider what it is that your client actually wants. Once you have figured this out then it will help you to create a message that appeals to that need directly and powerfully.

Think about this – value from a client's perspective isn't about you, your process or how you do it. It's about what they are left with when you have gone. How has their life changed? How is their business better? That's what matters. I read a great quote on the internet the other day:

"People want quarter inch holes – they don't want quarter inch drills." *unknown*

This is right on the money. Stop trying to sell them the drill and start explaining what a great hole they will be left with if they buy your product. It's about the hole not the drill. The value is in being able to hang a shelf on the wall when they are finished. While having a process is critical to being able to deliver value, the value to the client comes from the result of using the process and not the process itself.

So, as it relates back to your 5 second elevator answer to the question "What do you do?" it is critical that the answer identifies not really what you do but rather the value the client gets when you do it.

I have helped a lot of people figure out the 5 second answer and I will give you an example of a good one. Before I do, let me give you a few examples of some that started badly:

- "I help my insurance clients"…"Oh no! I am trapped in the elevator with an insurance salesman."

- "I write software to help clients"…"Oh no! I am trapped in the elevator with a software geek."
- "I perform financial analysis that helps clients to"… "Oh no! I am trapped in the elevator with an accountant."

And worst of all:

- "I am a consultant"…"Oh no! I am trapped in the elevator with a guy who just wants to steal my money."

Those are examples of bad statements because:

1. They are focused on what you do and not the value the client receives after you have done it.

2. Even if the guy was interested, he is going to refer you to someone else, more junior, in his company that "deals with that stuff" because it's not what he cares about as the business owner or senior executive. You lose the chance to connect to the decision maker and the one with the authority to write you checks forever.

One example of a great 5 second statement came out of a Dreamland™ session I was doing for a software start-up. They had written an application that medical clinics would use to convert paper records into digital and set up totally flexible work flows that each Doctor, Nurse and Administrator can design for themselves. When they started talking, I immediately got visions of dusty files and people inputting data. Not a compelling picture. So when I asked them to come up with the 5 second statement it started badly:

- "We provide software…"
- "We created a system to efficiently transfer…"

At this point, if I'm in the elevator with these guys I feel like I am having nine inch nails hammered into my head and the only way out is to hang myself.

So we stopped… and I asked the following three questions:

1. **Who are you trying to sell this to?**
2. **What do they care about?**
3. **How can you help?**

They answered:

1. **US based privately owned medical clinics**
2. **Making money and being free to practice medicine**
3. **Get the BS out of the way and make the first two happen**

"Great", I said, now we are getting somewhere. After a few tries we came up with the following statement in answer to the question "What do you do?"

"We created the **ABC process** that **always** triples practice **revenue** at a minimum, gets the administration out of the way, let's you **practice medicine** the way you want to and **gives you your life back.**"

This is a great 5 second statement because it directly addresses the need of the client. The "Value" that they will be left with when the process is complete. Do you see anything in there about software or medical records? Nope! So what is in there then? – let's look at the highlighted words:

PROCESS:

- This says you have a defined approach to whatever it is you do. It's tangible and not smoke and mirrors.

ALWAYS:

- This is a definitive statement of confidence and commitment. The word leaps off the page because nobody ever uses it anymore – the lawyers (drones in sector 7G) won't let you. We can use it because what we are creating is a statement of value, not a legal contract. You may not ever use this statement verbatim in reality but creating it will have allowed you to identify the real value you deliver. As a result, whatever marketing material or positioning statement you do use will be far more powerful. I know lots of people who do use their 5 second statement "as is" to great effect. You can add your conditions and modify the terms later, but if you can't get them to listen in the first place then there will be no "later".

REVENUE:

- "Show me the money!" This says that your process will impact revenue directly. Not canned MBA consulting that isn't connected to the money. We are focused. Money clearly isn't the only thing but nothing else your client wants to achieve will happen without it – Remember the mantra: *Fun, Fulfillment and the Creation of Personal Wealth.*

PRACTICE MEDICINE:

- Your client wants Fun and Fulfillment as much as you do. This statement tells them you understand that and, whatever it is, you will help them get back to doing it.

GIVES YOU YOUR LIFE BACK:

- Most Entrepreneurs I deal with got into their business in the first place because they were passionate about it. They worked night and day because they loved what they were doing and they were great at it. The result was rapid growth. Rapid growth brought the need to hire people and adding people turned the entrepreneur into a manager. Unfortunately, because they were so busy, they never fully transferred all of the accountability for running the place to the new people. So, they wake up one morning and say "What the heck happened to my life? Why isn't my business growing anymore? Why aren't I having any fun?" The "Gives you your life back" statement says that you can help them get that fun and productivity back again. Your process includes that as a key element.

A great 5 second statement will "always" hit on:
- **Process**
- **Money**
- **Certainty**
- **Client value** *(Your understanding of that value is critical in order to be able to get this part right)*

We created the 5 second statement as a way to force you to figure out what the value is you deliver to your clients and to create the core elements that quickly communicate it to people. Going back to the elevator scenario… remember the elevator? If the jaded guy in the elevator is a doctor and owner of a private clinic, then we have just hit him with a powerful value statement around what we can do for him. Even if he doesn't believe it for a second, it is so powerful and so on the mark relating to the value he is looking for, that he can't avoid asking the next question. This was always our goal when we delivered the 5 second statement in the first place. Getting him to ask that next question engages him in a conversation and gives you the permission to tell him how you do what you do – and how well you do it. We will now be using the Elevator approach to create the high level process you use to deliver the value and structuring the client message around it – an essential part in getting hired and paid by happy clients.

The question we want him to ask next is **"How do you do that?"** Crafting the answer to that will build the big blocks of our process in a way that can be easily explained to people.

CHAPTER FOUR
"HOW DO YOU DO THAT?"

How do you do that?

While you were delivering your 5 second statement the elevator went down a few floors and is continuing on its way. Our guy has been processing the outrageous value statement you hit him with and has come up with two conclusions:

- The first is that he doesn't believe that what you said you do is possible. Great! We've been successful in setting off every BS alarm in his body.

But…

- What you said is so powerful that, whether or not he believes you, he can't afford not to ask you the next question, just in case any part of what you said is true. He is compelled to just check and see if there is anything behind that 5 second statement.

This, of course, is exactly what we were trying to make happen in the first place. Getting the next question represents engagement on the client's part and starts the dialog – but you had better be ready to answer.

So the guy glares at you, takes a sip of bourbon, and says **"How do you do that?"** He is asking that question just to check and see if there is really anything tangible behind what you said you do and the value you claim to deliver.

The answer must not be longer than 15 seconds. This is not the time to get into detail – this is the time to outline the major "blocks" in your process in a clear and concise way. We just want to define the structure around how you do whatever it is you do and deliver the value you defined – proving it's not just smoke and mirrors.

I have found that, no matter what you do as a business advisor, it always fits into a four box delivery model. The answer to the question "How do you do that?" is, therefore, a summary of what you do in those non rocket science four boxes. The following is a typical and generic example. You will of course, adapt this to your actual program and make it more specific, but we have found that, language and technical details aside, the basics approach usually tracks this way in any consult… sorry, business advisory work:

1. DISCOVER/ASSESS:

- What is the client's vision for a successful outcome?
- Where are we today?
- What is the gap between the two?
- What are the main initiatives that will have to be completed in order to close the gap?

2. PLAN:

- Map the initiatives
- Identify the team
- Set the timeframe
- Create the project

3. EXECUTE:

- Assign accountability
- Launch project
- Initiate stakeholder stewardship. This makes sure that everyone who needs to know is always up to speed on where things stand and how it is going "Where we were, where we are, where we are going next"

- Identify and incorporate newly discovered Danger and Opportunity as the project progresses, i.e. "adjust to change as required."

4. ADVISE:

- Transfer your capability to the internal team *(always a popular concept with clients!)*

- Lock in the improvement achieved and make it "just the way we do business" forever.

- Conduct an ongoing Discovery/Assessment process to ensure ongoing improvement in line with an evolving client vision.

- Provide advice and support for the ongoing execution of change.

With the above in mind, the 15 second answer might be something like:

"The program is delivered in four stages with each one delivering standalone value. Stage one is clarifying your vision for the future vs. where you are today and identifying the main things that need to be done to close the gap. The second step creates an executable plan to get it done. We then execute the plan with full accountability assigned to people for getting it done. Finally, we take what we learned along the way and continue to make it better."

Not a lot of detail, but we have communicated the fact that there is structure around what we do. The point of this whole exercise in Dreamland™ (since we are not actually in the elevator with the client) is to help us create an effective and efficient process around delivering the value we have created, while we put ourselves in a position to be able to explain how we do it quickly and clearly.

This part of the Dreamland™ approach also starts to introduce the process for "continuing to get paid by happy clients". Note in the above four steps we made the statement that each one delivers standalone value. That means that the client only has to make the buying decision one step at a time. As you deliver each phase your credibility increases as does the client's trust in you. When you end phase one having identified the gap and required initiatives and having delivered your high level recommended action steps, the client's extremely likely to ask you to stick around and help them create the plan. We will talk more about how to make sure that happens a little later.

So at this point we have used the process to define:

- What we do
- The value it delivers
- The delivery framework in four main stages

Our elevator guy is now starting to warm up a little. The quick answer you just gave him has provided some comfort around the fact that there is a defined process in place, focused on delivering the value you outlined. He's warming up – but he isn't sold yet. Now he wants to get down one more level of detail to look at what is behind the process in the four boxes you described. What will you actually do to make that happen?

While you were giving him your 15 second answer, the elevator arrived at the lobby and the doors opened. As is always the case, (anyone who travels on business will know this!) in the elevator lobby there's a square glass coffee table and two couches facing each other. As you get out of the elevator, our guy looks at you and says "Ok, sit down… you've got five minutes to tell me how it works."

CHAPTER FIVE

"HOW DOES IT WORK?"

How does it work?

The answer to this question gets us down to the third and final level of detail required to properly describe your program and back up the value that it delivers. This five minute explanation provides the detail around what happens in the "Big Four Boxes" previously described. When I talk to people about this I suggest that, in order to answer it, they imagine the following: You have been hired to do the work and are approaching the client's office for the first time and are just about to walk through the door:

- What is the very first thing that you will do?
    - How will you do it?
    - How long will it take?
    - What is the output?

Then go through the same process for each part of the work to be completed in each Box until it is all accounted for. The point here – non rocket science – is that you know:

- What you are going to do
- How you are going to do it
- Why it is important

You are accomplishing four things by going through this process:

1. Creating a process that is easily understandable by someone else, will clearly represent a logical approach and increases their level of faith that you can actually deliver

2. Creating a process that will "Keep you honest" and make sure you tick all the boxes, while it allows you to focus on your client and deliver maximum value

3. Making it easy for the client to make the initial buying decision

4. Setting yourself up for perpetual employment

Having a process that other people can see, touch and understand is critical to their belief around how effective you are likely to be. The guy in the elevator is sick and tired of theory being touted by consultants.

- He likes the sound of the up front 5 second value statement
- The big boxes described in the 15 seconds make him comfortable that there is a "system" in place
- The third level 5 minute answer gets him over any further doubt

Having the process in place is critical in terms of getting the business in the first place, but the delivery of the actual value to the client doesn't come from the process. It comes from the ability to apply your talent to help the client. Point two simply means that:

1. You have created a process in order for you to get a client from A to Z

2. Along the way, following the process will make sure you tick all of the boxes as you go and don't miss anything

Remember Peter Falk as Columbo? For those of you who are

too young to have seen it or too old and have forgotten it, Columbo was a TV program about a rumpled but very smart Los Angeles homicide detective. As he finished questioning people and started to walk away he would turn back. There was always "Just one more thing", one more question that he appeared to forget to ask – that was always the killer question that wound up nailing the criminal. While that was effective for him, you really don't want any "Columbo" moments with clients. All of your clients will be different and you will focus more on some things with one of them and something else with another. In some cases you may skip a step in your process entirely because the client doesn't need it – but you will only do that after the process itself has caused you to look at the situation and make that decision logically.

As we look at this third level of detail, underneath the four big boxes, and you answer the questions we introduced earlier:

- What is the very first thing that you will do?
    - How will you do it?
    - How long will it take?
    - What is the output?

Here are some of examples of what the answers might be for each box. Again, these are just examples since your program will be unique and will contain its own elements and process. They are also based on the approach that might be taken by someone who works with clients on a generic advisory basis, focused on improving the overall approach to running a business. Hopefully, you will be able to see how this generic approach can be tailored to a specific situation that may be more technical or focused on a particular area of a client's activity such as Sales, Manufacturing, Human Resources, Finance and other "MBA" categories.

1. DISCOVER/ASSESS:

- Gather and review data prior to your first day onsite e.g.:
    - Current strategic plan
    - Financial package
    - Relevant operational data and key performance indicators
    - Organization charts
    - Internal audit or review documents
    - Any relevant reports and data connected to the work you will be doing
    - Current policy and process
    - Governance approach
- Conduct interviews with Owner, Executive and key stakeholders based on the insight you gained from your pre-work
- Take a look at the actual operation itself, "walk the floor and talk to the people" vs. what the owner, executive or management may have told you
- With your client's permission, talk to some external stakeholders such as clients they sell to and vendors they buy from. Is their view of the world and the relationship the same as your client's?

Example Output from Discover/Assess:

- **The "ABC Program" Assessment Report**
  - Your vision and view of the current state as you explained them to us
  - The understanding of the vision and view of current state as it was explained to us by all other stakeholders
  - Our direct observation of current state
  - Where they actually are vs. where they thought they were
  - Recommended immediate action

Completion of the Discovery/Assessment process:

- Provides standalone value and can be charged for by itself
- Sets you up for the client to say, "What's next and how are you going to help us?"

2. PLAN:

- Create the planning team representing all key areas/stakeholders that need to be included
- Clarify and lock down the three year vision
- Identify all of the issues that might stop us from achieving our goals
- Create the major objectives for each area:
  - Objective name
  - Description

- Success criteria
- Specific initiatives required to complete each objective
- Individual, "baby step" milestones that will get each initiative completed

■ Assign accountability for each objective:

- Who will leave this process "owning" the action related to each major objective in the plan?

■ Identify the payoff related to successfully achieving the goals – "What's in it for us if we can get this done?"

- Creates clarity around what success looks like
- Sets up communication around why we are doing what we are doing, that can be used with various stakeholders. Team members, clients, vendors, banks, press etc.
- Provides motivation for when the going gets tough, as it always does at some point

■ **Identify the client's strengths in support of their ability to accomplish their objectives "What is there about us and our partners that says we can get this done?":**

- The great things we have already accomplished
- The team we have built
- Our client relationships

- The things that differentiate us from others
- The clarity of our vision
- Our ability to execute
- The process we have in place to get this done

Example Output from Planning:

- **The three year, executable, strategic plan:**
    - Clear vision
    - Clear objectives
    - Specific initiatives
    - Assigned/delegated accountability for action
- Management & project framework in place in order to track progress and ensure success:
    - Project management process included as part of your output

The inclusion of a project tool for managing execution is also a powerful step in the quest for you to stay employed and to help the client with execution, as it:

- Is a graphic demonstration of all the work they will have to do. The process they can use to do it links you, in the client's mind, as an expert practitioner of that process - along with causing them to ask the question "How on Earth are we going to get all that done?" I actually had a client say that, and then they looked at me and said "You're going to help us right?"

In order to make this happen, we created a process and a tool called The Vision Transformer™. Sticking with our non rocket science theme, it's a simple and totally logical way to transform a strategic plan into execution. This approach has been used successfully for everything from start up operations, with no revenue or clients, through to Fortune 500 companies. It provides both a simple process for delegating accountability and a great approach for ensuring objectives are met. While we have created our own tool for this, the elements of it can be used by anyone and they are as follows:

- List all initiatives, grouped by MBA category (Finance, Human Resources, etc.)

- Assign priority to each one by giving it a simple color coded identifier:
  - Red = High Priority
  - Yellow = Medium Priority
  - Green = Low Priority

- Break each initiative down into Milestones:
  - Baby steps – so that each one on its own should be easy to do
  - Short, closed ended description of what is to be done. Closed ended so that there is no doubt whether it has been accomplished or not. So a bad milestone example would be "Think about the…" A good one would be "Identify the team required for…"

- Assign each milestone to specific individuals. There may be more than one person who will work on it but one person, and one only, must be accountable for it being completed

- Establish the completion date for each one
- Set up a colour coding system for tracking progress visually without having to actually read each completion date, as you review progress:
    - Completed = Blue
    - Not completed but on track to be done on time = Green
    - Not completed and in jeopardy if we don't take action = Yellow
    - Failed – past target completion date and milestone not done = Red

The colour coding approach may sound a little goofy on its surface, but we have found it to be very effective in project control and motivating the team:

- The overall change in colour, over time, tells a tale regarding overall success and progress
- Colour coding visually flags potential issues and calls attention to them
- Can be incorporated into project management approach and discipline:
- If it goes Red we don't just change the completion date and make it Green again
- If we decide to let a milestone go Red, because we are focused on something else, we don't just

automatically change the completion date and reset it back to Green, unless it is really a permanent change in priority and timing, we leave it Red so that it always reminds us that it is an outstanding item – "Look at me, I'm Red!"

- Always make it very clear what we should be concerned about and focused on, e.g. Red (high priority initiative) coupled with a Red (Failed milestone) is an obvious topic for conversation and focus

3. EXECUTE:

- Launch the plan - Team is clear on:
  - Objectives
  - Accountability
  - Timeline
  - Escalation process
  - Where to go for help
- Initiate the project management process:
  - Ensure progress is being made, track and enforce accountability
- Prepare the client for pushback from their team. Let's take an aside here for a bit and examine what we mean by this – because it is a critical element in you helping the client and staying employed:

We have all heard of the grieving process people have to go through when there is a tragedy – Denial ("This can't be happening to ME"), Anger ("Why is this happening to ME?"),

Bargaining ("God, if you get me out of this I will…,") Depression ("That's it, I'm done and there is no point in fighting it") and Acceptance ("Ok, these are my cards, so now what do I do?") Well, we have found that client teams we deal with go through their own "Five Stages" when it comes to coping with change and the process we are taking them through:

- **Skepticism/Cynicism:** They have seen the owner/company get enthusiastic before about change and new ways of doing things. This produces the "Here we go again working with a consultant, on the 'shiny penny' process of the month, that we will spend a lot of time on with no result" response

- **Testing:** Once they see that there really is a tangible process with a clear focus and worthwhile goal, they start to test and question it. Is it real? Is the company committed to it? How will it work?

- **Enthusiasm:** When they have tested it they cross over and become excited about what it might really do to change things for the better – for the company and for them (more fun to work there, better career prospects etc.)

- **Pushing Back on Accountability:** We find, especially in companies who have tried and failed to change in the past, that people don't understand what real accountability is. If you put a great project process in place, with clear accountability, then there is no place to hide and no way to deflect responsibility if things are not getting done. The clarity stops people from confusing and complicating the situation. The accountability for specific action means that there is never any doubt about who was responsible. At some point, as accountability sets in, someone on the team will push back.

- **Final Buy-In:** A good project plan will help people to work through the Push Back phase and start to see how their business and lives will be positively transformed. Once that happens, final buy-in occurs and the true culture change begins. This is when people start to ask for more accountability, because they understand how to make it work and that having it gives them freedom to act and control over what they are doing. This is also the point when new and creative ideas start to emerge from the team because their engagement and understanding is so much higher.

Having seen this a hundred times, we always prepare our clients for the **Push-Back**. How long it takes to show up varies around the length and complexity of the project, but it starts to rear its ugly head shortly after accountability has been clearly assigned, the project has been launched, the team is having to deal with real transition and change issues and they have been through at least two "project reporting" cycles. As human beings, they start to be worried about what happens if they fail. The symptoms of this appear as:

- People trying to complicate the execution we agreed on – "We can't do this, until we do that. Doing that is going to be complicated and takes some time so we will have to stop what we originally agreed on until we are ready to move ahead"

And the killer one for you:

- They talk to the owner/executive and start saying things like "Geoff is a great guy but I don't think this process will work for us – not sure he understands how we work. Maybe we should do this on our own or change the approach"

We see variations of this frequently, and expect them – it's just human nature taking its course. Preparing clients for this, and telling them what to look for as it emerges, is now a routine part of the project launch process we take them through. As a result, clients are ready for it, recognize it when they see it, understand it for what it is (push back against accountability) and know how to deal with it. Dealing with it is simply a matter of sticking to your guns and the project plan. While you are doing that, you are also looking for legitimately good ideas around how execution may be improved. That is a different "kettle of fish", is a very positive development and is dealt with in the next point. We have also found that, once clients get through this phase, people accept the fact that change has come to stay and get used to the new world – that is when positive culture change starts to bite in. Prepping the client for this, and helping them get through it, also means that you stay employed!

- Identify emerging dangers – things we hadn't thought about or that were not there previously, that we need to deal with. Recognize emerging opportunities – things we hadn't considered or were not there before, that we can now take advantage of:

  - As noted above, once the team gets through the Push-Back, they really start to get engaged. This is when new issues and opportunities are identified. The project execution needs to capture and incorporate all of them. It's important for the client because it means nothing will be missed. It's important for you because some of these new opportunities and dangers will relate to "stuff that should happen after this particular project is finished" that you will capture and talk to the client about as you move into Box Four – the Advice phase

- Initiate client stewardship reporting process – Keep the client informed about where the project stands vs. all of the goals. This process ensures:

  - Project stays on target
  - Critical decisions are made
  - The team gets recognition for progress and is motivated to keep going
  - You identify the next thing you can help the client with

For many of us, actually doing the stewardship report is a real chore – but it is critical to remaining employed.

The reason for this is because the report itself doesn't just let the client know where they stand on the project. It provides a constant reminder of the value they are getting from having you around. "How does that work?" We make it happen by using a simple Past, Present, Future bullet pointed stewardship report, and we do that for the following reasons:

1. It's easy to do
2. Bullet points means it's easy for them to read
3. The Past, Present, Future format reminds them of the value and keeps us employed:

    a. Past – this is where you were "Remember what a mess and how overwhelming that was?"

b. Present – this is where you are, now that we have been helping you for awhile. The progress is pretty amazing

   c. Future – this is where we are going next (if we are kept on to help) and that will be a very attractive place to be

I am not suggesting you patronize your clients. What you **are** doing with this report, while you update them on the progress, is reminding them of how things have changed since you showed up.

With perhaps one or two exceptions, all of my clients have been very smart people. In most cases they already knew what their problems were and what they should be doing about them. Their problem was finding the time to do anything about it or having the process in place to make it happen. That's what you, as an external advisor can provide, along with some specific technical capability in some cases. The stewardship report is a great way to help the client focus on the positive change that is happening because you are around. Not only will they appreciate what has happened already, they will start to think about what they might be able to do next – with your help. We had a client actually say to us "I don't know what's going to happen next but I want you guys at the end of the phone when it does."

Example Output from Execute:

- Employee/stakeholder engagement increases:
    - Willing acceptance of accountability
    - Seeking additional responsibility

- New ideas being generated – emerging opportunity and danger being identified, included and dealt with
- "Ownership" of the future being taken on
- Culture changing permanently
◾ Objectives being completed and goals being achieved
◾ Strategy evolving and clarity is created around next steps

4. ADVISE:

Although "Advise" is box four, you should actually move into it as soon as Execution has started and you deliver your first stewardship report. As noted, the stewardship report deals with past, present and future, so it gives you a perfect segue into providing advice on how to move forward. We are going to talk more about that in the next chapter.

◾ Initiate Client Stewardship reporting process:
- **Past** – quick reminder of where they were before project was launched
- **Present** – status report on current state, which:
  - Highlights progress
  - Deals with project housekeeping issues, what's working and what's not working
  - Identifies new opportunity
  - Identifies new danger

- **Future** – recommends action:
  - Dealing with danger
  - Leveraging opportunity
  - Evolution of strategy

- Transfer of capability from you to the internal team:

The transfer of capability from you to the internal client team is a critical element in continuing to be paid by a happy client – they love this part of what you do and it should also work for you in regard to your own business model around Fun, Fulfillment and Personal Wealth. This is true for two principal reasons:

Firstly, from the client's perspective, the transfer of your capability to their team adds real value, because it is increasing the permanent capability of their "Human Capital Assets". Recently there was a study done by an American university that included 3000 companies and compared the return on investment from money spent on increasing physical capital assets (bulldozers, machinery etc.) and that spent on developing people. The research showed that the investment in Human Capital paid off 3 to 1 vs. the money spent on "infrastructure". This makes perfect sense when you think about it. If you buy a new machine, no matter how well it is set up or runs, it will always have a certain maximum capacity to "do stuff". If you spend money on a human being then you are creating new skills along with the additional capability to "understand" the context of how things link together and work. This results in new ideas, creativity, increased productivity and leverage for you, forever. Unlike infrastructure, the human has an ability for infinite "software" upgrades and ability to continue increasing the value of their contribution.

Secondly, it counters one of the primary issues that clients have with hiring "consultants" in the first place – **"Once they get their hooks into you they never leave."** In this case, the client sees just the opposite behavior from you. It appears as if you are actively working to make yourself redundant by helping the internal team to replace you.

What you are **actually** doing, as you teach the team how to effectively use the process you installed, is preparing to move on to the next stage of value that you will be delivering to the client – leveraging of the improvement you have helped them to make. Think of it as a building construction project: you just helped them create a firm foundation and now you are going to help them build the ground floor. Each stage will be supported by the previous one and careful construction of each one will ensure that the whole thing survives as it grows.

So it works for the client. It works for you because you get to leave involvement in the mechanics of execution behind but, hopefully, stick around as a permanent advisor to the team whenever they need help. That means you don't have to stay connected to the time consuming day to day drudgery of the project, but you can still make some ongoing money from staying connected to it. In the meantime, you will be off working with the client on the next big opportunity now that they have the fundamentals covered and in play. This allows you to get back to the Fun, Fulfillment and Personal Wealth mantra surrounding the work you really love to do. Transferring the capability to the internal team frees up your time to focus on the higher value, more fun, work. Additionally, if you have associates working with you, you may be able to hand over the internal team to them and move away from it entirely. You pay them to do that work but also keep a percentage for yourself and that builds the capability for "making money while you sleep" What a great concept!.

- Identify the next action that the client should be taking – with your help

Using the Stewardship Reporting Process and other recommended tools, you will "get out ahead" of the client and be able to provide leadership and creativity that will be beneficial to them and keep you employed – continuing to get paid by a happy client.

By the way, remember that guy in the elevator? Just to refresh your memory, here is how I described him to you:

> **"He has a bourbon on the rocks in his hand, is rumpled, bent, folded, spindled and mutilated, jaded, bored and cynical. He has heard everything, seen everything, doesn't think he will ever learn anything new and doesn't believe anything he is told. The best salespeople in the world are constantly calling on him and he has seen every pitch in the book. Oh, and by the way, he just happens to be your perfect prospect.**
>
> **He doesn't care about you or what you do but his choice is to talk to you or just watch the floor numbers count down from 75 to L – talking to you wins by a thin margin… So he looks at you and says "What do you do?" Of course he doesn't really care what you do and doesn't expect to hear anything new or interesting – it's just that you are marginally more compelling than the elevator numbers."**

The process we have just gone through has converted him from this grumpy guy into a happy client who recognizes the value you bring and actually appreciates you being there. As noted, he recognizes the value you bring because you focused on understanding what he needed in the first place (Discover/Assess) and implemented a process that delivered it – the quarter inch hole, not the quarter inch drill.

Example Output from Advise:

- Updated strategic plan with:
    - Bigger vision
    - Clear new opportunity
    - Specific action steps
- Obvious opportunity for you to continue advising them – basically continuing to take them through your four boxes forever

CHAPTER SIX
CONTINUING TO GET PAID

Continuing to get paid:

Okay, let's have a quick recap of what we have covered so far:

GOAL:

Continuing to get paid by happy clients

STEP 1:

Realizing that it is pointless to get hired to do something you don't like doing

STEP 2:

Figuring out what you actually do want to get hired to do

STEP 3:

Creation of a process for doing what you do

STEP 4:

Creation of a simple approach for explaining the value you deliver and how you will make it happen

And… using it to get hired.

Before we go any further, there are a couple of points that need to be made:

1. Understanding what you want to do, creating a process for making it happen and being able to explain it are three components to getting hired. Actually getting hired will require you to wrap a sales approach around them. This book is not directed at teaching sales or sales process – there are millions of those – so I am not going to go into it, except to give you what I think is some excellent advice in this area. In almost ten years of successful business advisory work, I have yet to come across a more effective approach than that built by Dan Sullivan, creator of The Strategic Coach® Program. Strategic Coach's approach allows you to create prioritized and concrete steps, while transforming your business success.

As I pointed out, the world is jaded by the use of the term "value added" and yet identifying what that is from the client's perspective, and being able to position yourself as the one who can deliver it, is what will get you hired. Modern sales techniques seem to have created an almost adversarial or competitive relationship between salespeople and prospects – You will try to sell and they are prepared to defend themselves against it. No matter how sophisticated the approach is, most of them tend to be focused on better ways of explaining to the client how great whatever it is that is being sold, is.

Dan Sullivan has turned this on its head and created a process that initiates an almost instant relationship with a prospect and engages them in a conversation where they will explain very clearly what they are looking for. This allows you to simply explain how you will deliver that. For more information on The Dan Sullivan Question® and D.O.S.® visit The Strategic Coach® website. Dan's approach will also work for you with existing clients, on a long term basis, as a key component in continuing to add value long term and staying employed by them.

2. I gave you the "quick tip" of calling yourself a Business Advisor and not a Consultant. So while I said that you might think it was a goofy idea, it was directed at getting the client to ask you what the difference was. I think that there is a very real, powerful and…wait for it….non rocket science answer to that question. It's a powerful answer because it goes to the heart of what the client is going to be looking for, the value from their perspective:

- **The Consultant** is generally looking to find and solve a problem. Problems can be big or small but they tend to be self contained and generally closed ended. Neither of those things are going to be helpful in securing ongoing work

- **The Business Advisor**, first and foremost, wants to understand the client's vision and underlying strategy in order to figure out how they will harness their experience and process to help the client achieve them:

  - Every successful business owner or executive I ever met had a vision for themselves and their business but not very many of them had a good plan for getting there. That allowed me the ideal opportunity to build a relationship with them, while we figured out how they were going to get the plan in place and start executing it.

  - Lots of problems and opportunities fall out of the process you work through with a client in order to help them put a great plan in place. Because you are building the relationship, trust and credibility with them, once these issues and opportunities surface, you will have accomplished two things: First, they will recognize that they need help to move forward. Secondly, who else do you think they are going to ask to help them?

The key difference is the connection the advisor is getting to the underlying goals the client is trying to achieve, and not the surface problems they are facing in achieving them.

That results in a much deeper conversation and one that the business owner or executive is definitely going to want to have with you directly and not delegate to a junior or a technician.

A great example of the impact this approach can have, is the relationship that one of my clients, Brad Pickering, (**www.bradpickering.ca**) has developed with his Fortune 500 clients. In a market segment dominated by "Big Box" consulting firms, Brad works directly with the "C" suite and other senior executives around the creation and implementation of corporate strategy. This happened because, right from the start, he engaged those people in a conversation around the things that were important to them at their level. These things always represented big strategic issues or opportunities and were never "tactical problems" – large or small - that they would be delegating to more junior people. That ensured that Brad was able stay connected, add value and look for ways to continue to deliver leadership and creativity to people at that level.

Finally, I mentioned that, when things come easily to people they tend to think that it is just as easy for everyone and, as a consequence, they devalue it. Creating your package, using the process I have outlined in this book, will absolutely stop you from falling into that trap, because it will force you to clearly identify the strength of what you do and the value the client gets from it. As I have helped people through Dreamland™ and create their package, I can't tell you how many times we start out with them saying "Nothing I do is particularly special and I am not sure how I will ever get them to pay me to do it for them."

That is when I introduce them to the "Olympic Ice Skater" story. If an Olympic ice skater had the same view of what they do, and you asked them to describe how they execute a Triple Lutz, I guess the answer would sound something like this:

"There is really nothing special about it. I just skate very fast backwards, leap in the air, spin three times and land. No big thing…"

So I guess we can forget about:

- Getting the skating speed exactly right

- Keeping the angle perfect

- Knowing exactly when to "leap"… and being able to do it

- Controlling the speed and angle of the spin

- Landing exactly right

- The ten thousand hours of practice that went into learning how to do it

- The fact that 99% of the people on the planet could spend 20,000 hours learning how to do it (or me… 30,000) and still fall flat every time they try. That's the X factor called **TALENT!**

Great business advisors, **YOU**, are equally talented and creating your process will prove that to you and your clients. You have tremendous experience and can deliver significant help to the people who are struggling with issues and opportunities you know how to defeat and leverage. Your process will enhance your confidence and ability to get the business in the first place. Then it will allow you to put your full experience to work for your client ensuring that they will want to keep you around.

Okay. Now let's talk about the things you can do to stay hired once you are hired.

In order to help set the stage, let's look at two simple statements I heard from advisors recently. One said:

- "I get so caught up in the project I am working on that I forget to look for where the next work might come from".

The second said:

- "It's easy for us to get hired for the first phase of what we do for clients but they never keep us for phase two – they tell us 'Thanks, that was great, we have the ball from here'. We are very frustrated"

While this is clearly a problem for these advisors. it is also an issue for their clients. If the advisor is not looking ahead or paying attention to the logical next step, emerging danger and opportunity, then the client is not being well served. The advisor will come to the end of the project and the contract will end. The advisor gets fired and the client loses out on the value that should have come next. That's the worst case scenario for both of them. It's actually also a good example of a client being badly served by their advisor. In both examples the advisors are focused on "solving problems" and not advising.

The good news is that you can avoid these mistakes just by following the process creation and stewardship approaches we have covered.

Over and above that, however, I also have a couple of specific tools and processes you can use to help you do this:

THE FRONTSTAGE DASHBOARD:

In this example, the Frontstage is anything you do that is client facing and results in value for them and "Money" for you. The Frontstage Dashboard is a tool I use to make sure I stay connected to what my client is thinking, in order to make sure what I am doing (or want to do next) stays relevant. The process is quick and simple – but powerful, since it makes sure you never take anything for granted and always stay on top of what's going on around you. On an ongoing basis I ask myself the following questions and the answers go into my client action plan:

1. On a scale of one to ten, how would I rate my understanding of what is most important to my client right now? You can use any measure that makes sense based on the work that you are doing. I use Vision, Danger and Opportunity as my yardsticks

2. On a scale of one to ten, how is what I am doing, right now, relevant to what I know my client is concerned about or interested in

3. Sometimes the answers to these questions can be painfully clear. But asking and answering them is a critical step to keeping the client happy and writing

checks. So, once I have rated myself I set a 30 day target for each of them. So if, for example, I rated myself 5 out of 10 for number one I might set the goal of being able to honestly rate myself as an 8 in 30 days. This gives me a simple number as a target – not rocket science or calculus just an informed opinion of where I think I stand

4. The next step is to identify what I believe the top three things are that are on the top of the client's mind right now.

5. Then I set out the top three things I am going to do, with each of them, (so nine action items in all) in order to make sure I am having a direct impact on the things that are most important to my client over the next 30 days. If I had trouble identifying the top three things in step four then I obviously need to go "fact find" with my client. This is another great area where The Dan Sullivan Question® will help (**www.strategiccoach.com**).

Going through these five simple steps will:

- Keep you on your toes
- Ensure you stay relevant to your client
- Stop you from resting on your laurels and taking victory laps
- Help you to think through and create specific action steps to get it done
- Provide a "conscience" for you – did you do what you said you would do?

- Provide great content for the "Future" part of the Stewardship report

- Cause your client to say "Gee, how do you keep coming up with this stuff?"

THE CLIENT SERVICE MAP:

Following this simple approach will ensure that your vision for what is next is always out in front of the client's and that, consequently, you can provide the leadership to get them to go there. I designed it initially to make sure I stayed out 90 days ahead of my clients but the timeframe is irrelevant and will simply be driven by the nature of the work you are doing.

It works as follows:

Write down a short and clear outline of the initial work you have been hired to do – as soon as you get ready to start doing it:

- What is it?

- Why did they hire you to do it?

- What is the ideal outcome?

- What do you think (just a placeholder) the next logical step might be when you complete this work?

When you are nearing completion of the first 30 days work, or are at some other logical point, complete the Frontstage Dashboard and write down the answers to the following questions:

- What do they need to do next?

- How much time will it take?

- What benefit will they get out of it?
- What would I charge them to do it?

Then draft a preliminary communication approach that you can refine as you reach the 30 day mark (or other logical point) that you will start to use in order to nudge the client in that direction. If you start early enough, and use the right approach, they will be sold on the next step when you are ready to start executing it. They stay happy, you stay employed. The communication approach should be built around the following three key points:

1. What is the client benefit? If you clearly understand this then you can craft a message that identifies it for them

2. What will the investment be on their part "How much will it cost?". Rather than tell them that "my fee will be $xxx" I create a Budget for them that outlines the benefit, investment and timeline

3. The timeframe:

    a. When will we do it

    b. How long will it take

    c. How will it be done without disrupting anything else they have on the go

3c is always a critical point to address because "It's never a good time to do anything":

- We just hired a new CEO/CFO etc.
- We just lost our CEO/CFO etc.
- We are just going into our budget process

- We just completed our budget process
- It's our busy time of year
- It's our slow time of year (so people are either on vacation or out trying to sell stuff to someone)

You have to make sure you can take the objection off the table.

These are two specific examples of tools and processes you can use to keep the client happy and writing checks and they will help you a lot.

However, other than building a great relationship by doing wonderful work, the single best piece of advice I can give you is to really focus on the Client Stewardship process. The regular reminder of how bad things were before you showed up (The Past), how much progress has been made (The Present) and how amazing the future will be (The Future) is the most powerful thing you can do to ensure that happy clients keep wanting to pay you.

In parting I will leave you with my Ten Commandments for any great Business Advisor:

The Business Advisor's Ten Commandments:

1. It's all about your client – not you. The definition of value, from their perspective, is what they are left with after you are gone

2. Assume that your client is smarter than you are and understands their business

3. Start with the client vision – **then look at their numbers before you go to work**. Never wind up with a client who is the "Best organized company to ever go bankrupt"

4. It's all about questions not answers – asking & not telling

5. Be able to quantify the value you bring

6. Have process and tools, not just a sales pitch

7. Keep it simple and practical

8. Develop your next piece of business while working on the current one

9. Never take anything for granted

10. **Don't call yourself a consultant**

I hope reading this book has been a good use of your time and that these concepts, tools and processes will help you to build a great business. I am always happy to get suggestions for improvement from my readers and I am very interested in how any of you may have been able to put these techniques to good use.

Please feel free to contact me at **geoffg@thepacenetwork.com** I would love to hear from you.

GOOD LUCK AND HAVE FUN!

NOTES

Made in the USA
Charleston, SC
04 June 2013